I'm Reading About

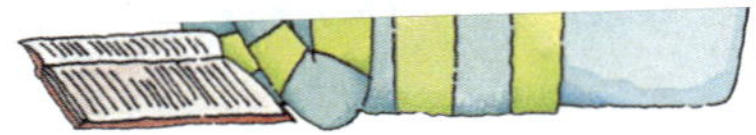

SOUTH CAROLINA

The Palmetto State!

GALLOPADE

by Carole Marsh

Printed and Manufactured in Peachtree City, GA., USA
www.gallopade.com

Book design: John Hanson

Editorial manager: Janice Baker

South Carolina is a great state.

It is one of a kind.

What makes South Carolina special?

Let's read about it and see!

NATIVE AMERICANS

Who lived in South Carolina first?

Native Americans did!

They moved around to find food.
They hunted in South Carolina's woods.
They fished in South Carolina's rivers.
They gathered fruits and seeds and nuts.

EXPLORERS

Some of the first explorers came
to South Carolina in 1526.
They came from the country of Spain.

Lucas Vázquez de Ayllón was their leader.
He and his men wanted to find new land!

SETTLEMENT

The first settlers came to South Carolina in 1670.
They built a settlement on the Ashley River.
They named it Charles Town.

South Carolina was one of the original 13 colonies.

Charles Town

STATEHOOD

South Carolina was the eighth state to join the United States of America!

Isn't it great,
to be a state!
I bet South Carolina
could hardly wait!

South Carolina became a state in 1788.

South Carolina

The 8th State

FLAG

I am the state flag.
I was adopted in 1861.

What colors am I?
Blue and white.

Look at me.
What else do you see?

I fly high over the state of South Carolina!

CAPITAL

Say hello to Columbia,
the capital city of South Carolina!

There is an important building in Columbia.
It is the State House.
South Carolina's laws are made there!

State House

SEAL

I am a seal,
but I am not the State Seal.
If I were, I would be very important.
I would be stamped on many official papers.
(Ouch, that might hurt!)

SOUTH CAROLINA
MARCH 26
JULY 4
QUIS SEPARABIT
MELIOREM LAPSA LOCAVIT
1776
ANIMIS OPIBUSQUE PARATI
DUM SPIRO SPERO
SPES

Now, that's official!

NICKNAME

State nicknames are fun!
State nicknames are great!
They share fun facts
about each state!

South Carolina's nickname is "The Palmetto State."

Many Palmetto trees grow in South Carolina!

The Palmetto State

BORDERS

Look at South Carolina.
South Carolina is in a region called "the South."

South Carolina borders two other states.

South Carolina was named for King Charles I of England.

Borders

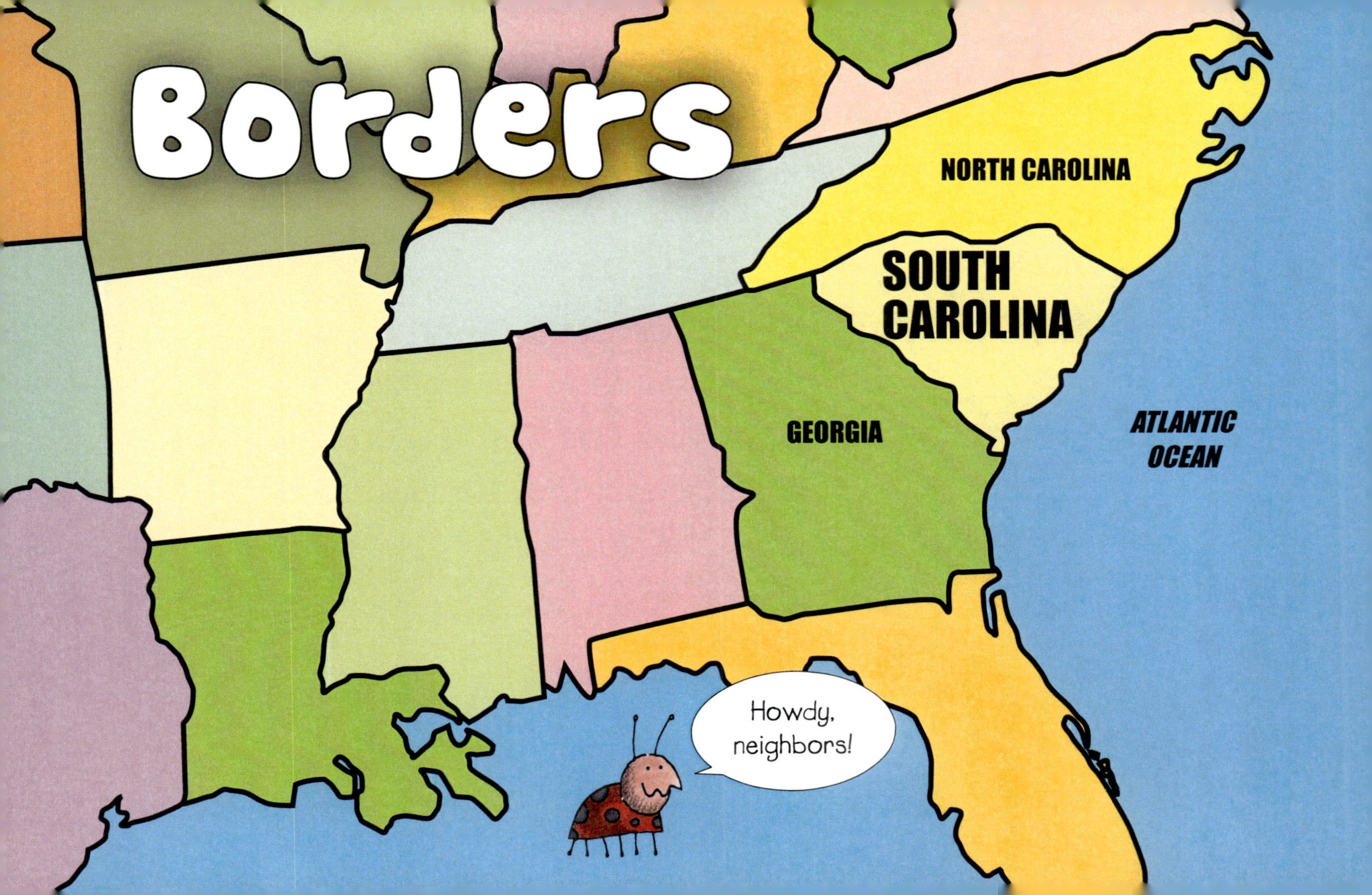
NORTH CAROLINA
SOUTH CAROLINA
GEORGIA
ATLANTIC OCEAN
Howdy, neighbors!

PRESIDENT

Andrew Jackson was the seventh President of the United States of America. He was born in South Carolina!

Andrew Jackson grew up on a farm. His home was near the border of North Carolina and South Carolina. He went to school until he was about 13 years old.

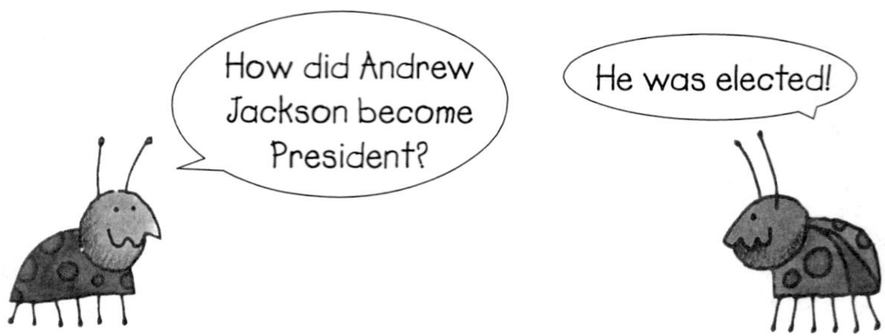

Andrew Jackson

PEOPLE

Many famous people

William Travis

Officer in the Texas army who died at the Battle of the Alamo

James Longstreet

General who fought for the South in the Civil War

Althea Gibson

First African American tennis player to win international championships

call our state home!

James Brown

Singer known as "The Godfather of Soul"

Jesse Jackson

Civil rights leader

Ronald McNair

U.S. astronaut

PEOPLE

Carolina Wren

I am the state bird, and I fly
over South Carolina, proud and high.

As I fly, up in the sky,
I flap my wings to tell you "Hi!"

The South Carolina state bird is the Carolina Wren.

BIRD

Yellow Jessamine

FLOWER

I am the Yellow Jessamine.
I am the state flower.

I grow where it's warm and sunny.
I climb over shrubs and walls.
I help make South Carolina beautiful!

Look at me! Smell me!
When I bloom, I turn fields into
blankets of yellow!

Palmetto Tree

TREE

I am a Palmetto—I'm the state tree.
Along the coast is where to find me.

My roots run deep, they keep me strong.
My leaves can be several feet long!

I stand up straight, big and tall.
Don't climb too high—it would hurt to fall!

Carolina Mantid

INSECT

I am the Carolina Mantid.
I am the state insect.

I am a praying mantis.
I have a skinny body and long legs.

I live on plants and shrubs.
It can be hard to see me.
Sometimes I look like a stick!

Atlantic Ocean

Let's go to the beach!

We can swim in the waves.
We can play in the sand.

We can build a big castle
where water meets land.

South Carolina's barrier islands are home to many animals:

Sea Turtles **Fish** **Birds** **Crabs** **Dolphins** **and More!**

BEACHES

Blue Ridge Mountains

MOUNTAINS

South Carolina's Blue Ridge Mountains
are the place to be.
Hiking, fishing, camping—
fun for you and me.

If you were to climb
to the top of a tree,
you'd have a beautiful view to see!

Salt Marsh

SALT MARSH

The salt marsh is a flooded area between the ocean and the land. There are many acres of salt marsh in South Carolina.

This habitat is home to many animals:

Crabs **Snails** **Mussels** **Birds** **Shrimp** **and More!**

South Carolina has more salt marshes than any other state on the Atlantic Ocean!

Fort Sumter

LANDMARK

Fort Sumter is a military fort.
It is a brick building with five sides.

The fort was built on a sandbar in Charleston Harbor.
It protected South Carolina from enemies.

The first shots of the Civil War were fired at Fort Sumter.

South Carolina Crops

AGRICULTURE

South Carolina has many farms.
Why?
Because South Carolina has good soil
and a warm climate!

Some of the top crops grown in South Carolina are:

Tobacco **Cotton** **Soybeans** **Corn**

Sports in South Carolina

SPORTS

Baseball! Basketball! Football!
South Carolina has it all.

Whether you like to watch or play,
You are sure to have a ball!

Panthers **Bobcats** **Tigers**

Gamecocks

& More!

South Carolina: Home of Myrtle Beach

CLAIM TO FAME

South Carolina is home to Myrtle Beach.
It is one of the most popular beaches in the country.

Visitors can stroll on the boardwalk.
They can also ride the Myrtle Beach SkyWheel!

Myrtle Beach has lots of sand dunes.
Tall sea grass grows on the dunes.

GLOSSARY

climate: weather conditions in an area over a long period of time

colony: a settlement ruled by another country

elect: to choose someone by voting

habitat: a place where plants or animals naturally live

laws: rules made by the government

permanent: lasting for a long time

region: an area that has similar characteristics

sand dune: a hill of sand formed by the wind near a beach

sandbar: a ridge of sand built up in an ocean or river by the action of waves or currents

settlement: the first community in an area